Keyholes

Poems by Doug Gillis

Images by Paul Gillis

Crooked Mile Press

Poems copyright © 2016 Doug Gillis
Images copyright © 2016 Paul Gillis

All rights reserved.

ISBN 978-0-692-70145-4

Published by Crooked Mile Press

Contents

The Loneliness of the First to Know 6
The Daddy Long Legs Spider's Way 7
Name that Tune 8
A Biography 9
This Little Light of Mine 10
Showdown at the Tidal Pools 11
Handsome Is 12
Itinerary 13
Finding Fuel 14
Vignettes of the Grand Design 15
Quasimodo Seeking Same 16
Choosing in the Multiverse 17
Dear Reader 18
We Still Have Judgment Here 19
To Those Who Wait 20
Fossils 21
Border Incident 22
News from Tuscany 23
Waiting for the Beloved Someone 24
Vivamus 25
Lazay Lay Bon Tom Roolay 26
But Answers He Got None 28
The Dizzy Season 29

Weather Report	30
Orders of Magnitude	31
Clocks and Yardsticks Rule, OK?	32
Reversals of Fortune	33
Dream Amnesia	34
RIP Somersville Town 1860 - 1904	35
Slow-Motion Afternoons	36
Full Spectrum	37
The Tree of Life	38
Snow Job	39
Assay	40
The Onset of Forever	41
Saying Goodbye in the Age of Discovery	42
Excavations	43
That Old White Magic	44
The Measurements of Uruk	45
The Neutral Zone	46

The Loneliness of the First to Know

As change impends and ends begin
emotions exit from their homes.
They swarm the neural neighborhoods
we made for them, and leave behind
cars upside down and statues flat,
and fires like footprints of the mob
converging toward some wicked act.

We wonder, seated opposite,
why our companion doesn't hear
the signature staccato pop
of words on automatic fire,
and doesn't recognize at once
in guarded eyes like furnace glass
the glow of burning covenants.

The Daddy Long Legs Spider's Way

This kind is often found indoors
walking on the ceilings and the walls,
a tiny ovoid balancing
on eight elongate and breakable legs,
segmented stilts that are filament-thin
with double knees and needle feet
evolved as if for a low-G moon.

He goes gingerly, probing the Way,
probing the void and surfaces ahead
like a blind man tapping with eight canes.
Periodically he halts and strokes
the air in ritual mode, shaping spells
and oracles or questioning a god.

When all the angles and omens are good
he hangs a crude, haphazard web
in a corner or behind a china hutch,
and still as scrollwork on a gate
he waits for something to jiggle the latch.

Name that Tune

Yesterday there was a sound,
a single note cut out of birdsong
or lifted from a shout,
and then repeated in percussive riffs
articulate of verve.
A nascency was trying to get out.

Today there is a different note,
extracted from a thunderclap
and then repeated, monotone,
as fusillade or bombing run,
inarticulate but understood.
A vacancy is trying to get in.

A Biography

The other night a lightning bolt
connected earth and sky
and stayed for the longest time
as if it were in a picture frame.
It marshaled blaze and thunderclap
in a towering long barrage.
It mastered all the space there was,
then in finale scorched its name
in capitals a mile high.
But even before the thunder died
the lightning and its name
were as gone as the mud-brick gods
that called the tunes in Babylon.

This Little Light of Mine

Finding myself in a darkened room
I struck a flaring match, and peeked
through its sequent keyhole views.

From fractions I imagined wholes.
By increments I tried to chart
the size and cargo of the room,
but the match burned short, abiding
no option but to let it drop.

I watched it go, a last ferry
receding fast, a Noah's ark,
its stern light dwindling in the dark.

Showdown at the Tidal Pools

The beach began at the parking lot
and dove between the sea-cliffs, expanding
fan-wise like sand spilling from a sack.
Between the low and high water lines
were volcanic rocks, coal-black and massive,
cratered with little pools refreshed by tides,
half-pint oases for life of pocket size.

In one of these we found a crab, boxed in,
without a crevice in which to wedge.
He faced us, half-in, half-out of water
with his back to the pitted wall.
We advanced a stick; he put up his claws.
We pulled the stick back; he put them down.
Advance, put up; pull back, put down.

Clearly he was good-to-go, a Leonidas
at Thermopylae, not thinking at all
of mercy or surrender or the need to weep,
and entirely up for an unequal fight.
In the end we saluted and withdrew,
ashamed perhaps for testing him that way,
and doubtful, doubtful, how we'll perform
when it's our turn and the Persians have come.

Handsome Is

Outside his window the winter night
has dolled herself in seductive black.
The stars are her sequins, the moon
the lamp she promised to leave on.
He hurries out the door, and there
winter carves out his lover's heart.

Sufficient stars still pit the sky,
but something has withdrawn.
The sky is dried-out honeycomb,
a skeleton like coral. He sees,
with accurate, animal eyes,
with corvine, pristine, lupine,
ferox, philosopher eyes,
the majority opinion of the stars.

Itinerary

The river is so serpentine
and slow, and you are so enthralled
by the pageant on the banks,
and by the floating likenesses
of sky and cumuli, that it must seem
there is no destination, only journey.

But then a sound insinuates.
From the lowest rung of hearing
it climbs without a pause: at first
a distant fizz, and then a drone,
and now a muttering baritone.

Inescapable, it will soon surround
and batter at your senses,
so loud that even you suspect
around the next curve is the cataract
and after that a plummet to your port.

Finding Fuel

On letters rubber-banded in a drawer
the ink is vivid but the meanings dim,
like flashlights that were on too long.
Remembered bonfires should be anodynes
against the chill and frostbite of decline.
But even though the letters reconstruct
with clarity the one who wrote them,
realizing even the inner charm,
even the gestures and the grin, even then
the picture of a fire does not warm.

Vignettes of the Grand Design

A spider seized a dozing locust.
She punched her venom in
then clung through kicking fits
until paralysis was full.
She dragged the passive locust
over stones it didn't feel
and down a crack in the world
to windowless cool rooms
where it will end its time
a bag of meals.

A matte-black military wasp
was hunting spiders crisscross
through tracts of thistle weed.
She caught one with her sting,
grappled it in her cargo sling,
then flew to a bunker under grass
where according to design
the only outcome is zero sum.

Quasimodo Seeking Same

Normally his journey to the bar
is untroubled by emotions.
He keeps them super-cooled.
Like atoms in a fluorine bath
they scarcely move,
but when excited by a stellar heat
they hypervacillate:
desire takes its turns with dread.

So he arrived not odd or even,
a hard-luck hunter
used to conies and defective deer,
pursuing with half his heart
a unicorn with her perilous horn.

Choosing in the Multiverse

Some say about a turning point
that each imagined act creates
a cosmos where that choice is fact.
Inside each greenhouse universe
the seedling act will ramify.

If plural cosmoses are real
and stream like bubbles from a pipe,
if bubble-like they intersect
sometimes, it would explain a lot:
the sudden darkening of mood
beneath a sky without a cloud,
the midnights prowled by silhouettes
that gesture, tease and tantalize.

Perhaps these visitations mean
that the one you loved is with you
but in a universe next door,
created on the day when here,
in this one, you turned away.

Dear Reader

From a layer of iridium we can read
that a meteor struck Cretaceous earth,
ejecting into the upper air a forest floor
and mountain range; they lingered there
as powder, drifting, dropping, worldwide.
The solar voltage dipped to lightbulb size
and Dinosauria's vigorous nations died.

Our record will be read, by beings unknown,
from a global sheet of styrofoam and tin.
Beneath it (but not above) will be the bones
of the *primus mobile* and artificer of his times,
who commanded the atoms under his feet
but could not command his appetites.

We Still Have Judgment Here

The watchful clock above the bar
is a judge par excellence of time
and sees the barflies wasting it.
His gavel taps the sentence out:
one thousand four hundred forty
vacant minutes in every day.

From minutes and intoxicants
the barflies craft eternities.
They craft illusions and then
inhabit them like movie sets.
But their eternities don't last.

Obligations orbiting the bar
keep coming due and coming near,
the way a dark companion star
periodically asserts its mass.
Tugged by such potent gravity
illusions waver and disperse.

The barflies bunker in, ignore,
drink more, ride with the tide until
the star goes by. Above the bar
the judge raises his gavel high.

To Those Who Wait

Heartache, like a Triassic lake,
submerges all in shoals and shallows.
For moments, or millennia, who knows,
the heart is steeped in sediments
and rolled around in calcifying streams
until it petrifies and gains that peace
that is so highly prized by stones.

Fossils

Soft parts are rarely fossilized.
So many conditions must be met,
so many coin flips land on edge,
for hair and brains to petrify.

Therefore how rare it was to find,
in situ, in an ancient seam
of tax returns and canceled checks,
the fossil of a vanished smile.

A coin had landed on its edge.
Perhaps one can, by sift and thresh,
by comb and clean, unearth someday
the rarer still, the fossil of a soul.

Border Incident

In the artificial twilight of the bar
the drunks were in their usual state
when a girl came in to use the phone.
She carried her much-brushed hair
the way an empire's best battalion
carries the colors through a border town.

The drunks were rattled for a while.
A few considered reform, and wondered
if there was enough lumber left in them
to reconstruct and start over again.
But most preferred the twilight after all.

News from Tuscany

A wedding pair who vanished
a few millennia ago
have recently been seen again,
together in the Etruscan tomb
where they were painted on the wall.

In buzzing spring, it is supposed,
in robes and lacy shawls
they were stepping through a dance,
as we do here in present time
to the same insistent notes.

The tokens on the wall persist.
The cosmos' song-and-dance goes on.
Under the floor, out of step
and out of tune, dance the fragments
of the real bride and groom:
nothing but atoms of lace and bone.

Waiting for the Beloved Someone

To only wait by moonlight is a risk,
a bet on double-zero in roulette.
Moonlight lacks the daylight's graphic traits:
color, shape, and complexity; instead
it offers shadow and ambiguity,
a place where anything could occur,
a place where someone can be waited for.
Possibilities conceal themselves
in the shadows between stripes of light.
Is someone there? Maybe yes. Maybe no.
Has the future gone off course? Maybe so.

Vivamus

Butter skitters around the frying pan
for seconds and is gone.

A mayfly that hatched at sunrise
reaches senescence by afternoon.

Transiting from seed to fallen log
trees remember in their annual rings
if they were hot or frozen, fat or lean.

Even mountains can be sanded flat
when rubbed by enough millennia.

And someday we'll see, on this same
continuum, the duration of you with me.

Lazay Lay Bon Tom Roolay

After a day hung over under office lights
the gloomy bar with its glowing fifths
could be the treasure room that lies
at the core of every well-built maze.
I claim my usual seat and coldly greet
the others who are aching to be whole.

Drink one exacts a spasm of disgust.
It is the entry fee, and in our brains
a seed of heat is quickened that compels
the smile we save for fealty in friends.
The heat performs its labors; it repairs,
connects and sutures with such skill
we feel a kind Gepetto has made us real.

We buy each other rounds of drinks,
we roll the Liar's Dice and laugh.
A jukebox dispenses histories to use,
feelings to have and characters to be.
We tell the truth with curlicues
and we ignore the pad, pad
of what we left growling by the door.

The regulars will someday speculate
why my stool is empty. Perhaps they'll say
I found the exit from the maze in time.
But I think they'll say I was reeling home
following the map I've made of curbs

and corners, and seeing starlight glitter
in the standing water I foolishly looked up
and fell to the galactic core, to stars
not wished upon, and vanished in the shine.

But Answers He Got None

What will we do
when the weather comes true?
What will we eat, what will we drink
when there's nothing but heat
and the reservoirs sink?
Where will we go, who will we be
when there's nowhere for snow
and there's nowhere to flee?
What will we do
when the future comes true?

The Dizzy Season

In March in cold white skies
when winter is pivoting to spring
birds align on telephone lines
like iron filings on a magnet.

From time to time when nothing
but nothing is happening
the birds all quit the wires at once.
Commanded by an unseen magnet
they loop-the-loop in cold white skies.

Weather Report

Today golems are made of silicon, not clay;
they run on electrons instead of spells.
But just as in antiquity they have no souls.

And just as mages summoned demons up
with a whiff of sulfur and a price to pay,
so in our day greenhouse gases rise to heaven.

The golems say the earth is cooking in its skin.
Some species' clocks have speeded up, so prey
and predator don't meet on the appointed day.

When warblers migrate north too soon
they're not at home when the budworms hatch:
the budworms forage like a biblical curse.

Where the sun chews out a small Sahara
mice continue their accustomed routes
and leave their bones like abandoned tents.

While bees remain in their winter doze
the flowers bud and bloom and die sans issue:
impatiens, immortelles, forget-me-nots.

Such deaths, occurring under rocks,
in ponds and treetops, are data in a trend:
for many the Begats are coming to an end.

Orders of Magnitude

A trillion suns in the nighttime sky
float on the surface of a water drop.

Inside the water drop is an ocean;
one-celled fishes swim within.

The mind can plumb a nucleus
or step across the universe
or live forever in a single day.

Clocks and Yardsticks Rule, OK?

An event as rare as meteors commenced
when a bully chose me from the crowd:
the familiar world began to stretch.

The local objects of creation realigned
around our axis; he at his end snapped
in focus; lookers-on were smeared around.
The earth's rotation stopped and time divided.
His footsteps fell in slow stalactite style
while I sprinted to Neptune's moons and back.
I lobbed grenades and mortar shells
that popped without effect around his head.
I rang all the bells but no one heard.

And so between each incremental step
a thousand outcomes effloresced and died.
At last physical law and *force majeure*
defeated prayer, magic, and fair play:
the clocks all chimed at the expected time,
the bodies met at the expected place.

Reversals of Fortune

The storm arrives, reminding one
that flesh survives in a paradise
between the interstellar ice
and the open oven of a sun.

The democratic rains, that drown
the kitten with the sewer-fly,
and jewel the wino's dying eye,
are in possession of the town.

Persuasive currents sweep the streets
where converts to non-being pitch,
a rising fetid flood, on which
the world's reflection vacillates.

Just as the drowning soul agrees
to sink, a calm rewinds the view:
flights of birds like fleurs-de-lys
cross an infinity of blue.

Dream Amnesia

I woke up with the persuasive sense
that a sweet dream had just hurried off
leaving nothing but its shape behind.
It was like the ground where a rare
elusive animal has lain all night
and left a hollow there. I was bereft,
but of what or whom I didn't know.

RIP Somersville Town 1860 - 1904

The coalfield town has disappeared
but some of the inhabitants stayed on,
congregated in the graveyard
where the miners housed their dead.
On the headstones chiseled names,
dates and epitaphs summarize their times.

Death was familiar then: death-dates often
are clustered around a shared event,
an epidemic or a powder blast,
and the many cherubim attest
that childhood was unsafe.

Death wasn't final then: across the gulf
in low-relief the living and the dead
shake hands in greeting and farewell.
They converse through epitaphs.
"I'm Happy in Heaven," say the dead.
The living say, "I'll Be With You Soon".

The headstones, weathered and hard to read,
will keep eroding until they are smooth
and can't convey what the miners knew.
And so the conversations end, and so,
although they know, the dead can't say.

Slow-Motion Afternoons

According to the script, as clocks pass noon
our shadows stage a slow and soundless fall
to concrete surfaces, and lie full length.
Like movie heroes shot through the heart
but dying gracefully, they still have time
to explain and regret and take it back,
to see with clarity before the fade-to-black.

Full Spectrum

Raindrops striking water spend themselves
in diminishing rings until they are smooth.
Fireflies flash on and off just long enough
to signal "Hello, I'm here," then disappear.

Our time is also short, but we crave more:
an afterworld visible in wavelengths
only the dead can see, as bees see
in ultraviolet the flowers that they need,
as snakes find their prey in the infrared.

The Tree of Life

Yesterdays fall to ground and rot,
vanishing from substance
and vanishing from thought.

Tomorrows, still on their stems,
are drilled by worms
and softened by disease.

We crave an end, but not today.
Today we crave another fruit
to eat from the sickened tree.

Snow Job

Moonlight prettifies the lethal snow
which then like glitter glue
entraps our gauzy notions as they launch.
Their wings beat out a Mayday,
then decline, then decay
till only dingy stains remain.

It will be clean again.
From an infinite train of winters
the snows will disembark,
will gape like country visitors
beneath marquees of neon stars
announcing that the savant moon
now performs her sleight-of-hand.

It will be clean again and again.
Only in our wrinkling hearts
will be knowledge like a stone:
that there has been a neat transaction,
dingy stain for gauzy notion.

Assay

By day the highway towns are built
of scuffed-up bricks and cinderblocks
where strangers live unpolished lives.
Nightfall changes all: along the road
the lights of their houses and streets
are gemstones heaped within our reach.

Pebbles too are gemstones in a stream,
but once picked up they dry earth-toned,
as lusterless as those scuffed-up lives
behind the bricks. No spark. No glow.
But they are gemstones even so.

The Onset of Forever

His fingers quit scribbling the words in air
that stammered in his head unsaid.
His lungs inflated a last few times
and eons stretched between each breath.
His swiveling eyes abruptly stopped,
having found what they were looking for.

He changed between two ticks of the clock
and lay there disengaged, a mimic
slyly like the man we knew, but dead.
Outside the room the ruckus and hum
of Earth's biota never missed a beat.

Saying Goodbye in the Age of Discovery

Being neophyte Conquistadors that year
we mapped the *terra incognita* of L.A.
The map she made had towns and contour lines
and details of the tribes that came first hand.
My map was inferential and mostly blank.
On it she was the "Here be Dragons" sign,
the spices, silk, and ivory, the Inca gold
and ambergris, and a grant of wide domains.

She chose a café that had a foreign look,
with olive trees, statues, and tiled walls,
and tables with mosaic tops around
an indoor fountain with a weeping fall.
I tried to broadcast cosmopolite cool
but apprehension fizzed inside my skin.
Beneath her jaunty guise, beneath the flair,
foreknowledge was the subtext in her eyes.

She spoke the lurking words and then set sail
and sailed beyond the margins of my map.
Her words resounded off the patterned walls,
reverbed diminuendo out windows and doors,
then rose through wisps of cirrus clouds
to sound's far barrios and border towns
where still they go, diminuendo round and round.

Excavations

At Warka now the style is cinderblocks,
not bricks, without the bas-reliefs of gods.
Radios instead of horns announce
the wars of the Koran and ballot box,
and tanks maneuver on the sands that hide
the highest stair step of the ziggurat.

At Uruk IV they found the unglazed bricks
shattered, where the god's apartments were,
and bones of priests and of the warrior caste
diminished in the dust, and beyond the gates
the famine-scalloped mummies of the poor.

At Uruk V the ziggurat was new.
War chariots maneuvered on the sands
and men were marching to the compass points,
armed and armored and eager to erect
the thrones and temples rising in their minds.

The pit is now too deep and too far back
for artifacts. At nightfall high above
streetlights open their diamond eyes,
unwinking and hypnotic, like the stone
set in the Lugal's curse-protected crown,
towards which the hands of dead men stretch.

That Old White Magic

The letters that remain, except for one,
I salvaged from our personal Atlantis.
Some potent magic lingers in the ink.
When I reread them the other day
a stone-dead mummy woke,
unwound the cloth, and touching me
with her youthful hand she said
"I loved you then. I love you now."

The final letter, separated
by our two lifetimes from the rest,
referred to stories we were in,
but carefully, like a pianist
playing the sweet notes only.
She forgave me entirely
for severing our lives, but now, for us,
there would only be Atlantis.

I bent my head. I felt the ice crack
after centuries of freeze.
I cried because it wasn't yesterday
and then because it was.

The Measurements of Uruk

The stumps of ziggurats
and the flattened walls
describe the city's size,
how high, how wide,
but only the clay tablets tell
how much Inanna loved Dumuzi.

The Neutral Zone

I note gratefully while walking by the quay
how a church piled up from stones is veined
with black branches and no leaves; the way
a dove's public groaning is ugly and maimed;
how soft, furry, rotten, pilings get
from lake water clapping, licking of their trunks;
how some ducks sail out yet
some in a brown rush flush their banks
when footsteps shake them; how smoky night
clamps down, and fixes the lake, the bird,
the church and branches in still smoky light
like an old daguerreotype. Seen or heard,
unharmed by me, they dredge no secrets up,
no eyes that stare, no words that never stop.

www.ingramcontent.com/pod-product-compliance
Lightning Source LLC
Chambersburg PA
CBHW022345040426
42449CB00006B/731